S0-ECN-262

Homework — And Why

by
David A. England
and
Joannis K. Flatley

Library of Congress Catalog Card Number 84-62988
ISBN 0-87367-218-6

Bloomington, Indiana

This fastback is sponsored by the Northwest North Dakota Chapter of Phi Delta Kappa, which made a generous contribution toward publication costs.

The chapter sponsors this fastback to demonstrate its support for the Phi Delta Kappa Educational Foundation and to promote its goal of stimulating discussion of educational issues.

Table of Contents

Introduction 7

What Do We Know About Homework? 13

How Have Educators' Views on Homework Changed? 13

What Kinds of Homework Do Teachers Assign? 15

What Reasons Do Teachers Give for Assigning Homework? 16

What Do Students Think About Homework? 17

What Types of Students Are Most Likely to Do Homework 18

How Much Time Is Spent on Homework? 19

What Are the Effects of Homework on the Improvement of Learning? 19

What Are the Problems Facing Teachers and Students Regarding Homework? 20

When We Talked With Others About Homework 22

What Ought We Be Doing With Homework? 31

For Principals 32

For Teachers 33

For Parents 34

For Students 35

Homework Do's and Don'ts 36

Some Questions We Should Be Asking About Homework . . . 39

Bibliography 41

Introduction

Melissa is an eighth-grader. Because she is involved in sports and other extracurricular activities, she does not get home from school until around 5:00 p.m. on most afternoons. She helps prepare dinner and has other household responsibilities. It is often 7:00 p.m. before she begins her homework, and she frequently spends two hours or more per night on her lessons.

Bob Preston and James Blackburn have children in the same elementary school. James is on the road for his company an average of three days a week; and although he strongly encourages his son to make good grades and helps him when he can, there are many nights when he is gone. Since his divorce, he has hired a housekeeper who stays over when he is away. Bob, on the other hand, is home every night. But he, too, is unable to help his son, for both he and his wife are functionally illiterate.

Jim Harrison has been a high school principal for 15 years. He has seen the public expectation for "lots of homework" rise and fall over the years. His teachers believe "parents expect it." But fewer than 40% of the students in his school live with both parents; one-third have part-time jobs; and another third have a least a 45-minute bus ride to and from school each day.

Betty Johnson has been teaching social studies for eight years. She teaches five periods daily, has three different classes to prepare for, and has an average of 32 students per class. Although she regularly works more than 12 hours a day, she is still unable to grade or respond to even the 160 homework assignments she receives each *week*, let alone the homework she might assign every other day or so if she could keep up with it.

Exploring homework, and some of the "why's" behind it, is the central purpose of this fastback. As the anecdotes above illustrate, we believe there are problems to be addressed when the subject of homework is considered, just as we believe there is frequently a need and justification for homework. At the very least, there are improvements to be made in the way schools handle homework, and we will be making recommendations toward such improvement in a later section.

Borrowing from the definition by Bond and Smith, who have been two of the important investigators of the topic of homework, we define homework as "tasks that the child is assigned to do on his own time, after school hours, as an extension of his classroom work. It is usually distinct from the multitude of extracurricular activities or intellectually stimulating activities undertaken voluntarily by students." Given this definition, it would be difficult to argue that what Abe Lincoln was doing by the light from the fireplace was homework. Indeed, homework as defined above may leave little time for exploratory, self-chosen reading or for using home computers, watching something worthwhile on television, or even for talking with one's parents or other adults. But we do wonder whether Abe Lincoln would have found time to become the man he became had he been assigned three hours of traditional homework each night.

Contemplating Abe by the firelight is useful in that it suggests that homework can as easily get in the way of developing knowledge and wisdom as it can enhance one's education. Either way, for as long as there have been schools, there have been teachers assigning, parents encouraging, and children bemoaning homework. Like bells, recess, buses, chalkboards, and report cards, homework is and long has been a tradition in our schools.

Just how that tradition has evolved concerns us less than what it portends for today's students. That is, given the contemporary contexts of schooling, given the nature of the non-school lives our children now lead, and given what we know about how learning takes place, what cases can be made for and against homework? Do we dare suggest that we have reached a point where we should consider doing without homework altogether? Maybe, just maybe, we should. However, it is not our intent here to offer a diatribe *against* homework.

To suggest eliminating homework or even requiring less of it is to fly in the face of currently popular public wishes. Responses to Gallup Poll questions of recent years reveal that the public favors more homework for students. For example, the 1978 poll found that five out of seven people who suggested ways the schools could improve specified "more homework," and a year later the same poll asked parents to reveal what they liked best in their child's school. The assigning of "lots of homework" was frequently mentioned and equated with "high standards." Also there have been recent and widespread sentiments that our schools are not doing very well, although the 1984 Gallup Poll reports that public attitudes toward the schools have taken a more positive and perhaps a more sympathetic turn. (It would be interesting to know if increased homework can be related to more positive public perceptions of our schools.)

For some, calls for increased attention to basic skills means increased time for skill-and-drill work, and that in turn can lead to more skill-and-drill work at home. Moreover, making schools "tougher" has been equated with increased homework. In the 1984 Gallup Poll on education, the public was asked: "Do you think students in public high schools are made to work too hard in school and on homework or not hard enough?" In 1984 the percentage of respondents who said "not hard enough" was 67%, compared to 54% in 1975. What this question assumes is that homework is a part of "working hard in school."

Recently, there have been calls for lengthening the school day and increasing the number of required academic subjects – more English, more math, more science – all intended to raise standards. These changes affect class scheduling. For example, in several states and in many schools instructional periods are being *shortened* so that more required courses can be fit into each semester. When classes are reduced from 55- to 45-minute periods, the lost 10 minutes may have previously been used by teachers to begin – or more fully explain – homework. When schools shift from six- to seven-period days, there is little question that the school day is becoming more crowded. Already, we can observe that fewer and fewer schools provide in-school time for study. Study halls are becoming less common. Therefore, at the same time that the need and expectation for homework increases, time to get started on it or to finish it in class is much less available.

Next, let us consider factors in the lives of students today that influence how much homework is done. For instance, more and more students have part-time jobs after school – more today, in fact, than at any other period in our history. The increase in two-income families requires parents to rely on older children to look after younger children at home after school. For many children, access to quasi-educational resources at home is much more common than for children of even 10 years ago. Adolescents and younger children are enticed by video games and home computers, and by the ubiquitous television. Still another time-stealer is shopping malls, which are overrun with adolescents.

Wealthier kids have time and money for flute lessons and gymnastics lessons; less affluent kids may have to work part-time or help out more at home. Such traditional activities as church and scouting groups still compete for youth energies and time. Now, more than ever before, the competition for youngsters' time is intensely keen.

At the same time, more and more kids return home from school to empty houses. The phenomenon of latch-key children has to be considered in this discussion of homework, as does the many parents who are less and less able to help much with homework, even if they are available. Assisting with drills on multiplication tables is one matter; helping children with metric conversions or with mastering the writing process is quite another story.

It is important for both parents and educators to have a realistic sense of these contexts in which homework takes place – if it is to be done. These contexts – some educational, some social, and some economic, cultural, and developmental – clearly influence how students will respond to homework. And they are at once complex and interrelated. Moreover, the contexts and environments for homework are changing on these several fronts simultaneously. Kids are changing. Family life is changing. The schools themselves are changing. But homework assignments just keep coming; they even may be increasing. Too often these assignments are just taken for granted and remain unexamined.

Because of the current contexts in which homework is done, several problems are inevitable. Foregoing discussion of the very worth of homework for a later section, let us assume that homework is of some benefit. What problems can merely assigning homework create?

First, if homework is assigned, there is an attendant expectation by students (if by no one else) that someone will "check" the homework. Just what checking homework means can vary from teacher to teacher. If the situation is at all like that of Betty Johnson, the social studies teacher described at the beginning of this section, checking mountains of homework assignments on a regular basis may mean going through it to acknowledge that it was done, and that responding to it in any meaningful way is an impossibility.

It is also safe to assume that some kids are more likely than others to do homework when it is assigned. Brighter kids, who are already excelling in school, are more likely to do their homework than slower kids, who are having trouble in school. It is those kids who are getting the least out of the school day who could probably profit most from completing some school work at home. Yet, it is those very students who, for a variety of motivational and socioeconomic reasons, are frequently among the least likely to do homework at all, and even less likely to take homework seriously. Basing grades on a student's inclination to do homework is a common practice that is likely to create a problem. And making mastery of subject matter reliant on a child's ability or motivation to work at home may be creating even more serious problems, not to mention widening the gap between academic achievers and underachievers.

Then, too, kids need some time to be kids – which is more than a kid's argument. As some interviews that we have conducted reveal, homework may be dominating family discussions before, during, and after the evening meal. Just getting kids to do homework becomes recurring ground for major battles in many homes. In the background, we hear chants of "Teach them discipline!" and "They must learn life is demanding!" We would submit that taking cold showers teaches discipline, too; and, compared to doing homework until 11:00 p.m. three or four nights a week, it would probably do more to keep kids awake in school. As for learning that life is demanding, perhaps being in school seven hours a day is demanding enough. And if it is not, having the school day encroach on what might otherwise be family time may not be the best solution.

At the risk of protesting too much, we state again that we are not necessarily *against* homework. But because we have been thinking a good bit about some of the issues related to homework, reading about what is known regarding homework, and talking to a variety of people who have to deal with homework, we do see some problems worth exploring and some questions worth asking.

The following section reflects the "homework" we did to answer the question, "What Do We Know About Homework?" We review some of the research on and thinking about homework that others have done. Then, we share several of the "real voices" we heard as we talked with parents, teachers, administrators, and students about homework. The number of people we talked with in each group was quite small, so we make no claims that they represent a scientific sample. Our purpose was simply to sit down and talk with people who are caught up in homework, although from different perspectives. Our hopes that these discussions would be provocative were fulfilled.

Finally, our thinking and reading and talking about homework has convinced us that the ways teachers assign homework, the type of homework they assign, and the purposes for which they assign homework can all be improved. We also believe that schools should have some consistent policies regarding homework. And there are some things parents should know and be advocates of when it comes to homework. We conclude with some recommendations that should make us all better informed as we deal with "homework – and why."

What Do We Know About Homework?

In reviewing what researchers and others have said about homework over the last 70 years or so, we found shifts of emphasis regarding homework. Yet much has remained constant. In Knorr's *Synthesis of Homework Research and Related Issues* (1981), he points out that homework, despite changing views, has been an accepted and expected part of American schooling. Nevertheless, there has been little sound research on this subject. The minimal research that did exist on homework suggested a positive relationship between homework and achievement (Hedges 1964). However, in 1979 both Harding and Friesen reviewed the research on homework from 1900 on and found no clear-cut evidence as to its effectiveness. Simply stated, while schools have historically endorsed the assigning of homework, there has been little data supporting, or refuting, its worth as a means of improving school performance.

Approximately 500 articles on homework have been indexed since 1900 (Knorr 1981). Most have focused on three general areas: 1) educators' views of homework, 2) influence of homework on students, and 3) research on homework. In exploring these general areas, we shall raise some questions followed by some answers suggested by our reading of the literature.

How Have Educators' Views on Homework Changed?

In the first half of the twentieth century the majority of homework-related research focused on describing types of homework activities. The types identified were primarily practice and preparation assignments. Also during this time some research activity concentrated on the effects of homework on primary grade children.

Beginning in the mid-1940s, educators showed less concern about homework and put more emphasis on extracurricular activities. After the hectic period of World War II and the Korean War, time that had been spent on homework was more frequently devoted to after-school clubs, sports, and student volunteer organizations. However, this emphasis on student activities shifted abruptly after the successful launch of Sputnik in 1957. Among many other changes this technological feat imposed on American education was an immediate re-emphasis on homework. Math and science courses were stressed, colleges raised admission standards, and homework was increased. During this time, homework was viewed as a means to an end, and that end was academic excellence (Check 1966; Wildman 1968). During the early 1960s, more and more homework was emphasized because Americans were still reacting to the space race with the Soviet Union.

In 1966 Good (Knorr 1981) concluded that no homework should be given in the elementary grades *unless* a child wants to do it. He contended that homework for young children is inappropriate and counterproductive. While Good and others stressed student interest as the primary justification for homework, the practice of assigning homework remained essentially unchanged. Homework was used either to provide drill practice of a concept or to prepare a student for the next day's classwork. Homework was assigned regularly to fulfill the above purposes. It was considered a necessary component of education.

The social ferment during the Vietnam era of the late 1960s had an impact on many aspects of education, including homework. Many educators believed that schools should place more emphasis on the mental health aspects of education. Too much homework, therefore, was thought to apply too much pressure on students. This position is reflected in the following quote from a committee of the American Educational Research Association in 1968:

> For mental health, children and young people need to engage in worthwhile out-of-school tasks suited to their individual capacities. Homework should supply such tasks and reasonable freedom in carrying them out. Whenever homework crowds out social experience, outdoor recreation,

and creative activities, and whenever it usurps time devoted to sleep, it is not meeting the basic needs of children and adolescents.

This trend emphasizing students' social adjustment and emotional development, which continued into the 1970s, was not, of course, unlike the "life adjustment" philosophies of the Forties and early Fifties. Now, as we progress through the 1980s, we are awash in the back-to-basics rhetoric. Homework is once again viewed as a means toward academic excellence and as a means of instilling discipline in students.

In even this brief consideration of homework in the past 70 years, it is not hard to see that views have ranged from homework being perceived as thwarting emotional and social development to homework as a means to academic excellence and disciplined minds. It should be noted that these trends toward more or less homework have been a response to popular attitudes and popular educational philosophies; they are not a response to old or new research on what homework accomplishes and how it influences children.

What Kinds of Homework Do Teachers Assign?

According to LaConte (1981), historically homework has been assigned to practice skills taught that day in school or to prepare students for the next day's lessons. Such homework usually consists of drill, memorization, and reading assignments.

Research on the amount and nature of homework conventionally divides homework assignments into three categories: practice, preparation, and extension activities. Homework assigned for the purposes of practice or preparation usually takes the form of written assignments, reading, drill work, or individual work. Only the last of these suggests assignments that are intended to remediate an individual's particular weaknesses or to strengthen certain skills.

Extension activities usually take the form of either long-term projects or problem-solving activities. Long-term projects are usually an extension of topics covered in class. Examples are drawing a Mayan calendar, building a pyramid, or cooking a pilgrim meal. These assignments are usually self-selected and are carried out by small groups or by individuals. Problem-solving activities may require several days to several weeks to complete. They typically are done in small groups and require students to take the responsibility for investigating a current social or scientific problem.

Depending upon the kind of homework assigned, certain outcomes can be anticipated. From LaConte's (1981) review of the literature, he suggests that practice/drill homework (by far the most common) may cause students to become bored with school. He also suggests that assigning the same homework to the whole class may not be effective. A further finding in his review suggests that homework is most effective if it is matched to the ability and knowledge of the individual student. But such assignments are also known to be the least common.

What Reasons Do Teachers Give for Assigning Homework?

According to Bond and Smith (1966), there is rarely a consensus within a school on how much homework should be given or when it should be assigned. Also, there is little consensus among teachers as to the reasons for assigning homework. LaConte's review identifies five standard reasons given for assigning homework. Bond and Smith cite similar reasons in their research.

The first reason is that homework teaches self-discipline; that is, by doing work independently at home, students learn responsible behavior. It assumes that time management, self-direction, motivation, and application are automatic by-products of homework. This reason also assumes that all students need help in the area of self-discipline.

The second reason teachers give for assigning homework is that it eases time constraints on the curriculum. When teachers are given a curriculum guide at the beginning of the school year and are urged by the district office to cover it by the end of that year, they feel that if some of the content can be covered through *homework*, more of the curriculum can be completed. (This reason is very appealing to world history teachers.) It becomes, then, the students' responsibility to "teach themselves" some segments of the course content. This reason for assigning homework assumes that all students can read the text and assimilate the information independently. Even if the assignment is discussed the next day, the students are still largely responsible for learning some of the course on their own.

Third, it is thought that homework teaches independence and responsibility. This reason is similar to the first and likewise suggests that homework is not so much a means of learning subject matter as it is a vehicle for learning responsible behavior. It also implies that homework can be used to foster independent inquiry.

The fourth reason teachers give for assigning homework is that it supplements and reinforces school learning. This rationale stresses the need for drill and practice to ensure mastery learning. In this sense, students are not learning any new material but are reviewing what was learned in class.

The fifth reason focuses on the bond that some say is created between school and home through parent participation in homework. LaConte's survey of the literature cites studies that correlate increased positive relations between home and school with the increased practice of assigning homework. The research suggests that homework provides a common ground for communication between parents, students, and teachers.

Reasons for assigning homework may vary, but most teachers do assign homework. Check (1966) surveyed 1,016 individuals, including students (elementary through college), parents, and teachers. His research revealed that 89 out of 90 teacher respondents favored homework, a majority of university professors encouraged homework for public school students, and 38% of school-aged students favored homework with certain conditions. Although research in this area is scant and not particularly definitive, it is consistent: homework is not only expected, it is valued. However, the *reason* homework is valued will vary.

What Do Students Think About Homework?

Coulter's (1980) research suggests that while students do not regard homework as having any intrinsic value, it is regarded as a necessary part of schooling. Earlier research by Check (1966) supports this finding. In Coulter's research with elementary through senior high school students, 80% of the students surveyed thought that homework was necessary. Interestingly, he also noted that the highest ratio of negative responses to homework came from children whose parents are professionals.

While the majority of students accept homework, there are conditions that students say influence their willingness and inclination to complete it. In Kerzic's (1966) survey of middle school pupils, 76% indicated that their homework was more manageable when they had a clear understanding of the assignment, when they had all the necessary materials to complete the assignment, and when they had a quiet place to work. In this study, Kerzic also noted that 91% of the students indicated that they required some help in doing their homework. In sum, while most students consider homework to be an integral part of schooling, they also state the conditions that are required to complete homework successfully.

What Types of Students Are Most Likely to Do Homework?

In our review of the literature we found it interesting that almost all types of students say they do at least some homework fairly regularly. Check's (1966) research reports that public and parochial school students do not differ in their participation in homework activities. In a more recent study, Coulter's (1980) data suggests that low achievers participate as readily as high achievers. He also notes that socioeconomic background is not a variable influencing homework participation, a finding we found surprising.

Although there is research suggesting that all types of students engage in homework activities, other research (LaConte 1981) indicates that more homework is given in classes where the teacher perceives greater academic ability. Also, students who come from supportive families tend to be given the most homework to do. How *well* (i.e., conscientiously, competently, and consistently) students of differing backgrounds actually perform homework tasks has been given very little attention, nor has the nature of homework assigned to different ability groups.

How Much Time Is Spent on Homework?

Knorr's research (1981) indicates that homework usually begins in the fourth grade. As a student progresses through school, the amount of time spent on homework increases, a finding confirmed by numerous studies. In the middle grades (6, 7, and 8) Kerzic (1966) found that the average time students spent on homework was 62 minutes a day. By the ninth grade Coulter (1980) found that a third of the students in his study spent *no* time on homework, but 15% spent more than two hours a day. A synthesis of several studies shows that most students claim to devote between one hour to 1½ hours a day on homework. Coulter noted a dramatic increase in the amount of time spent on homework between the 10th and 11th grades. Up to this level, time spent doing homework appears to remain fairly constant, from one hour to 1½ hours a day.

LaConte's review reports that girls spend more time on homework than boys and college-bound students spend more time on homework than non-college-bound students. LaConte states that a point expressed repeatedly in the research is that teachers think that their assignments take less time than they actually do. Hence, a recurring theme in the research is the inaccurate teacher predictions regarding homework time.

What Are the Effects of Homework on the Improvement of Learning?

Friesen (1979) summarized the results of 24 research studies dealing with the correlation between homework and academic achievement. These 24 studies were conducted between 1923 and 1976 and included both elementary and secondary schools. The results of the studies analyzed provide neither supporting nor refuting evidence regarding the effects of homework on learning. Also, Harding (1979), in reviewing the homework research from 1900-1979, was unable to find clear-cut evidence proving the effectiveness of homework in improving pupil performance.

Although most research does not provide statistically significant correlations of homework with general academic achievement, there is recent research indicating a positive effect between homework and math achievement (Cartledge and Sasser 1981). LaConte (1981) notes this research does suggest that math homework may improve performance in older students particularly. Yet, there appears to be no research showing that this is true in other content areas.

Knorr (1981) has suggested that because there is neither a common definition of homework nor any consensus on constructs by which to conduct research on homework, educators are forced to make decisions regarding its use without help from a sound research base. This could be because the limited number of studies that have been done have not had adequate experimental designs or adequate definitions of terms.

What Are the Problems Facing Teachers and Students Regarding Homework?

There are several problems connected with homework assignments that could offset any positive effects that homework might have. Bond and Smith investigated homework in 116 schools and discovered that in more than 50% of the classrooms all students were given the same homework assignments. This practice suggests that students who may have mastered the content are doing the same work as those who have not. LaConte corroborates this finding in his review of other studies and argues that blanket homework assignments may not be effective.

Bond and Smith's research also revealed that in 66% of the school districts surveyed, the teacher did not systematically correct, grade, and return homework. In the same survey only 3% of the teachers were required to use the results of the homework assignments in determining report card grades.

Kerzic (1966) surveyed 748 intermediate school students and found that 91% needed some help on their homework. This help ranged from explaining directions to working through the entire assignment with the child. Kerzic also noted that 75% of the students surveyed indicated that interruptions, uninteresting assignments, and television were the three most common factors detrimental to homework completion.

We know there are other problems related to homework. However, few have been explored thoroughly in research and other professional literature. For example, there is no evidence that teachers are provided any training for when or how to assign or to respond to homework. Homework may well be taken for granted in teacher education just as it is in public schools.

It is safe to say that, beyond our common experiences as assigners of, doers of, or grumblers about homework, we really know little about its effects and benefits. Not only is there relatively little research on homework, what there is has failed to establish a strong and consistent link between homework and achievement. What we can be more certain of is that homework is an accepted part of schooling, that homework practices are seldom analyzed, and that problems resulting from sometimes chaotic and unreasonable homework assignments are common to parents, teachers, principals, and students.

We leave this section somewhat in the same frame of mind as we left the literature we read in preparation for writing about "What Do We Know About Homework?" We are not convinced that much of substance *is* known; and if readers of this section have been persuaded that there is a good knowledge base out there, we have conveyed more certainty than we intended. Our sense of the literature on homework is that it is vague, uncertain, sometimes contradictory, and perhaps even thin – and this is unfortunate given the ubiquitous nature of homework in our schools.

While we may have failed to enrich or extend our knowledge by looking at homework-related research and literature, we are much more pleased by what we learned from dozens of conversations we had with parents, principals, teachers, and students, whose comments provide the content for the following section.

When We Talked With Others About Homework

In this section we include some of what we learned in conversations about homework with parents, principals, teachers, and students. Again, we are mindful that those we talked with do not necessarily represent a typical cross section. Still, we did do some modest "designing and selecting" of our sample. For example, we tried to talk to approximately equal numbers of parents, principals, and teachers, and children at three levels: elementary, middle school, and high school. Of the 20 students we interviewed, about half were female; some were excellent students and some were weak students; but *all* seemed to have much to say on the subject of homework. Principals and teachers we talked with came from schools reflecting socioeconomic and racial diversity. Of the 15 principals we talked with, five were from private schools, as were six of the 20 teachers. Finally, the 20 parents (or sets of parents) we interviewed were stopped randomly in food stores. (In the name of "science," however, we approached potential interviewees in three different food stores and at various times of the day and week.)

We did use some questions consistently, as the following review of what we found will indicate. At the same time, open-ended questions allowed respondents to follow their own impulses. Our interviews with parents averaged about seven minutes in length, with teachers and principals about nine minutes per interview, with students around 12 minutes each. So much for our "methodologies."

As one might predict, there were certain views common to all four groups. Even more predictable is that there would be differences of opinion – and certainly there were. Students expressed consistent views, for example, in response to the question, "What comes to mind when you first hear the word 'homework'?" But the student responses were not consistent with those of parents, teachers, and principals.

Several students, of course, said things such as "Yuck" and "I hate it!" and "Do we *have* to talk about it?" But most ended up saying at one point or another, "I guess we have to have it." Homework seen as a necessary evil was a common point among several students and among some parents. One high school sophomore told us, "It's one of those things you grow up hearing is 'good for you. In some classes, I wonder why – what good does it really do? I usually feel guilty when I don't do mine, or copy someone else's." (More on that "copying" point later.)

Principals indicated to us that parents "expect it." One elementary principal stated, "We may be giving too much too early. But later on, kids have even more; and we have to start easing them into it." Another said, "I wish we could get by without it altogether. But there's no way now, I guess." She went on to add, "My own children complain about homework. To be honest, I can see why at times. But they do it." And still another simply stated, "Homework is part of the school experience. When it is assigned, it is to be done."

Although parents often indicated an acquiescence to the realities of homework, they did not always express pleasure with homework as it is assigned. One ninth-grader's mother summarized sentiments expressed by several parents when she offered, "If they assign it, the kids just about have to do it. It's often very hard to make ______________ do her homework. Sometimes it is so hard to see the value. But we do it." Another parent just said, "They assign it because they feel it is necessary. To do well, you have to keep up with it."

We were most surprised by the number of teachers who said they wish *less* homework was necessary. When teachers were asked to share the first thing that comes to mind when they heard the word "homework," more responded with comments expressing their concern with the amount they felt they had to assign than with anything else. An eighth-grade math teacher said, "A lot of days I wish I didn't have to give them so much for at least two reasons – half of them can't or won't do it, and I have trouble doing justice to the half who do turn in their work." He continued, "I feel the curriculum and the texts are such that I should really give them even more homework than I actually do."

Two teachers in the same school expressed quite divergent viewpoints, although both assigned plenty of homework. One said, "I have to assign it. Homework is essential. It is a given." A colleague, though, stated, "I wonder if I could teach as much and as well and if the kids would learn just as much if I never assigned homework. It is such a hassle, and I have a lot of questions about the value. But I assign my share."

The majority of parents, principals, and teachers agreed that homework is "good for the mind." Not surprisingly, fewer students agreed with this viewpoint. Parents of older students often suggested to us that homework is a good way to "keep them in at night." And the mother of a fifth-grader said, "I probably couldn't get him to do any homework if it was not for the TV. Our rule is, No TV till the homework is done."

At least one principal at each level used the word "discipline" in describing the value of homework, and virtually all we talked with agreed that homework is linked to good grades (a point, by the way, which many students we talked with would dispute). A seventh-grade English teacher said, "When they do their homework, they demonstrate some responsibility to the course. Doing homework I assign is largely a demonstration of effort."

Here, too, though, there were occasionally dissenting opinions. Several of the parents' comments suggested some doubts about the values and positive benefits of homework, particularly in light of the effort and time expended in doing it – and in the parents' case, seeing that it was done regularly. Most administrators, on the other hand, seemed to agree with the middle school principal who said, "To do well in school, children just have to do their homework." Among teachers, there was less consensus here. A young language arts teacher offered a more elaborated view, and one that would clearly contradict the prevailing administrative philosophy we encountered: "For a child to achieve good grades, he or she generally must complete homework when it is assigned. But that does not necessarily mean that doing homework, however consistently, results in academic growth."

To be sure, there were staunch defenders of homework among teachers and parents. Others, though, see homework as too often consisting of busy-work. And the quality and nature of the homework teachers *do* assign was discussed specifically by at least some we talked with from each of the four groups. An eighth-grade social studies teacher said, "Maybe if we felt compelled to teach less, they would learn more. Maybe if we gave fewer homework assignments and made them more meaningful, more learning would take place in class. Maybe. I just don't know."

To recount much of what students said about the general values of homework might offend the reader. But three comments, in particular, are worthy of contemplation. A tenth-grader said, "Just looking like I am doing my homework keeps my parents off my back and gives me enough to turn in the next day." A third-grader said, "Homework must be good for me or Mrs. ____________ would not be upset when I didn't do it. But sometimes I don't do it and she don't know." And a high school senior said, "When I think about all the time I spend on homework, I am amazed. I am just amazed."

In reconsidering all the discussions we had, we were perhaps most surprised to find that *only the principals* consistently argued that homework is academically essential. But one principal did make distinctions between types of homework: "The real issue is probably what we ask students to do at home. The worth of different types of at-home studies is something we should know more about."

Complaints about the nature of homework are common among parents. The parent of an eleventh-grader complained, "One teacher has him doing an outside report a week. I know no one really reads them, and my son knows it, too. What he's learned is how to use information in an encyclopedia and make it sound and look fuller and richer than it really is. But he caught on to how to use encyclopedias for school work in the fourth or fifth grade." A fourth-grade girl took a different and more direct approach to the same general problem: "Sometimes she gives us thirty problems to do. That's too many. Ten sound OK. But we never get just ten."

Other students said things such as: "Homework can be OK if it is not too often or too much." "It makes sense when doing it helps you the next day or on a test." "Homework is easier to do when I know the teacher will look at what I have done." These, then, appear to be some of the conditions under which homework makes the most sense to the students with whom we talked. To summarize, the mother of an older student told us, "Homework for its own same sake is a bad idea. My daughter feels negatively about all homework assignments now, as a result of having had to do too many senseless ones." Only rarely could students we interviewed think of specific homework assignments they thought "really mattered" or that they "didn't mind having to do."

One of the more instructive questions we asked turned out to be, "What is the major issue or problem with homework?" What interested us in these responses was not only the variety but also how parents, teachers, and principals defined the problems differently.

For principals, the most frequently discussed homework-related problem was their attempts to satisfy parents that sufficient, but not excessive, homework was being required by teachers. We surmise that part of the problem stemmed from attempts to satisfy two groups of parents: those who believed that teachers were not requiring enough homework and those who called to complain that teachers required too much or that what they required was only busy-work. One high school principal estimated that calls about the *amount* of homework far outnumbered calls about the *nature* of homework assigned among the one or two homework-related calls he reported receiving each week.

From our conversations, we determined that there is more concern at the elementary level that not enough homework is assigned than there is at the higher levels. An experienced private elementary school administrator told us, "You can look for some parents to start expressing concern at about the second grade. The questions are general ones, such as, 'Is my child challenged?' I have come to think that the real issue is homework, and the increasing desire for more of it."

We were surprised to find many more teachers suggesting that time to grade or evaluate homework was a greater problem than getting students to do it. Both issues were mentioned often, however. A young social studies teacher was already beginning to fall into what he called the "assign it, sign it, and let it slide" pattern, which he used to resent in other teachers.

Teachers at all levels expressed some concern about their inability to handle the paper load that is generated by homework, particularly the one-to-one feedback or instruction that completed homework assignments may reveal is necessary. As for motivating students to complete homework, one sixth-grade instructor spoke for several others when she stated that student willingness to do assignments at home was not the major battle. The greater problem, we learned, was encouraging students to do their homework "well," which she proceeded to define as "conscientiously and thoroughly." Even some of her better students, she said, acted as if they believed "just getting it done any old way is all that matters."

Parents as problems – more than as partners – were mentioned, too. Parents of both persuasions ("give them more" and "give them less" homework) can lead to tensions or misunderstandings between home and school. "What do you do," an English teacher asked, "when a kid says, 'But my Mom helped me proofread it,' after the child has turned in a paper filled with mechanical and spelling errors?" Another situation was described by a math teacher who said, "I have marked an entire page of problems wrong and assigned a '0' for work done at home. Then I learn that Daddy has either done the work or 'helped' with it." The notion that homework strengthens home-school relationships is not always the case.

Although their inability (whether due to time or competence) to help with homework was mentioned by parents we interviewed, there was more to suggest that the number one homework-related problem for parents was "seeing that they get it done." Phrases such as "constant battle," "door slamming time," and "it wears me out" were among those used to describe domestic homework scenarios.

As always, there were the predictable differences of opinion regarding appropriate amounts of homework. Some parents, of course, believe there should be more and that the lack of homework is indicative of a problem. On the other hand, the parent of a high school sophomore said, "I think ______________ gets frustrated because he knows even if he sits down to do his lessons very early some evenings, and stays right with it, he still can't do it all. And some of what he does I know he just flies through." Another parent offered, "Teachers should have to do all the homework they assign, as well as the assignments assigned by the kids' other teachers. If they did that for a few evenings, things would change in a hurry."

Boys and girls naturally resent the encroachments that homework obligations make on their time for other activities. For example, a high school senior said, "I haven't had time just to 'read read' during a school year for a long time." He defined "read read" as reading in pursuit of his own interests and tastes. The suspicion that if homework were reduced the majority of kids may spend more of their new-found discretionary time in shopping malls or watching TV may miss the point. Homework can take a great deal of time – time some kids would "waste" but time other kids would use more profitably.

Several students spoke directly to the purpose and value point. "Most homework is busy-work," said one seventh-grader. Asked to define what "busy-work" was, he said, "just what it says – stuff to do just to keep you busy." The following view from a ninth-grader represents several similar statements from students we talked with: "In most classes, it is a joke – a game. Sometimes you can just hand in anything and get away with it. Handing it in or showing it seems to be the idea."

Assessments of how much homework was actually reviewed by teachers ranged from "zero" to "almost all," with most students reporting that more *was not* reviewed or checked than *was* reviewed or checked. Several students expressed displeasure when homework is not returned, and our post-interview impressions were that teachers were more likely not to return homework than they were to return it. One eighth-grade girl said that the teacher "who makes a check in the grade book, and that's it" was typical in her experience.

Finally, a half-dozen kids mentioned cheating as a major homework-related problem. "It's easy to cheat in a lot of classes, and everybody does. But copying someone else's homework to turn in when nobody looks at it really doesn't seem like cheating." A sixth-grader confided, "It's just easier to pay to have it done. You know – fifty cents for your math. This one kid is probably dumber than me but he does all the homework. He fails some of the tests. And I pass some."

In summarizing the major problems we heard discussed, it would be reasonable to say that for principals the primary homework problems arose from conflicting parental expectations; for the teachers it was most often students' conscientiousness and the teachers' time; for parents it was seeing that homework was completed; and for the students it was whether time spent on homework was justified in terms of its perceived purpose and value.

We collected a good bit of information, limited though our sample was. Certainly our perceptions were broadened, deepened, and, we hope, enlightened. What we have tried to do in this brief report is to reflect some of the major themes we heard from the various groups who discussed homework with us. Admittedly, we may not have exercised perfect objectivity in selecting which quotes we used. The ones we shared herein struck us as being particularly provocative and, if nothing else, much fuller than the sometimes monosyllabic responses or off-hand remarks one learns to expect in any such spur-of-the-moment interview. For the most part, however, individuals in all four groups seemed both ready to talk and armed with opinions.

Regardless of how we reflect on and subsequently share what we learned, a somewhat less than rosy picture is painted overall. We began our exploration with an idea that there are certain problems related to homework in the schools; we ended our interviews finally convinced of it. We know from the strong sentiments we encountered that there are obviously dissenting views. There *are* homes in which homework is not an issue, and not just because it is ignored; there *are* teachers who assign homework judiciously and purposefully; and there *are* principals who insist on it, parents who support it, and students who do it. But in each of these cases we feel we are referring to the exceptions, not to the rules.

We did receive some excellent and explicitly stated ideas as to how the assigning of homework might be improved. We can add to these several sensible recommendations made by others who have written about homework. We shall try to pull all of these ideas – from real kids and parents and teachers and principals talking to us, from our own ruminations, and from our reflections on others' ideas – into our final section, where we offer ways we think homework could begin to make more sense.

We have tried to establish that there are problems and questions. Some have to do with the amount of homework assigned. Some have to do with the nature of homework assigned. Some have to do with parents' and students' attitudes and expectations. We know now that identifying the problems related to homework is much easier than providing workable strategies for alleviating the problems. In our concluding section, we turn to that much harder task.

What Ought We Be Doing With Homework?

We have been thinking and reading and talking and hearing a great deal about homework recently. As authors of this fastback, we think our attention to homework is rather uncommon. Despite the fact that parents, principals, teachers, and students deal with homework almost daily, there is little discussion of its value and even less solid research evidence. As we have tried to establish, there are many problems related to homework. However, we believe that there are ways in which homework can be utilized more effectively. We offer, then, some suggestions to principals, parents, teachers, and students as to how homework might be dealt with in more productive and rewarding ways.

We are not so naive as to argue that our modest suggestions will make homework a joyous event in students' lives. Nor do we think all confusion about its purposes and values will be eliminated. And we certainly would not suggest that homework assigned, as we would have it, will increase learning in our schools. But no one can argue convincingly that homework, as it currently exists, accomplishes any such goals, either. The supporting research is deficient. Our recommendations are, in the main, based on common sense. We suggest that homework, as we would have it, may positively influence some students' inclination to do it and to do it well, no more and no less. But that is probably enough – and our disclaimers are by now most assuredly sufficient.

We begin with general recommendations for each of the four groups concerned: principals, teachers, parents, and students. These general suggestions will be supplemented by specific lists of "Homework Do's and Don'ts" for each group. We conclude with suggestions as to the kinds of questions we feel need to be pursued by research on homework.

For Principals

We begin with principals. Our first recommendation is that principals become primary advocates for general, schoolwide policies regarding homework assignments. Is there, for example, *ever* justification for a child to be assigned more than 30 to 45 minutes of homework on a single night for a single class? We think not, and we would therefore argue for establishing reasonable, schoolwide limits on the amount of homework. Second, we suggest that principals assist faculties with some interdepartmental planning of homework assignments and schedules. In middle and senior high schools, especially, it should be quite simple to establish Tuesday and Thursday as the nights math and science teachers assign homework, and Mondays and Wednesdays as the nights social studies and English teachers assign homework. The next week, the nights could be reversed. Certainly, adherence to such an agreement would take some planning by the teachers; but maybe part of the current spate of homework problems results from too little planning or planning that takes into account only one class at a time.

We would further suggest that principals be mindful of who is assigning what kinds of homework and of how much is being assigned in their schools. It would be a good idea for principals and for counselors to be aware of any long-range or extended projects a given teacher may require. We think principals should know which teachers are inclined to assign rather heavy amounts of homework every night and which teachers assign none. Such information would, if nothing else, make responding to parents' and students' complaints much more informed.

These latter ideas suggest that building administrators begin talking with teachers about homework and expressing an interest in the nature and amount of homework students take home. To do less is to assume that teachers "just sort of know what they are doing" or that they "sort of find their own way" with homework. Anyone with a memory or with kids in school knows better.

For Teachers

Teachers, in turn, should be able to outline daily homework assignments a week in advance and provide students with written descriptions of all long-term or extended course projects well in advance of due dates. The ways in which homework assignments will be evaluated and factored into grades should be made clear to students and to parents and should reflect those general schoolwide policies we feel should be established. Certainly, homework expectations will vary from teacher to teacher, but planning and clarity of assignments should be givens.

A letter to parents early in the year explaining homework policies and major projects may change parents' misperceptions of teachers when children say, "He never gives homework" or "She just assigned the novel tonight and I have to have it read day after tomorrow!" Seldom are these the cases, but often these are the reports. Who knows for sure unless the teachers make their policies and plans clear to parents? Students forget when it comes to homework. And they exaggerate.

The notion, however enticing, that teachers can consistently base homework assignments on the actual needs, interests, and abilities of individual learners is probably unrealistic. As ideal as such a goal might be, we know that it could work for only a very few teachers. There are simply too many children to allow for the kind of individualization that would tailor homework for each learner in a class. This is not to say there is not a place for differentiated homework assignments for certain groups of students or for certain instructional purposes.

We believe it is reasonable that teachers have a clearly established and defensible purpose for every homework assignment they give. Teachers should be able to say, "Doing your homework tonight should help you to . . ." and then provide answers that are more related to instructional goals than promises of "improved grades" or "a longer recess." Finally, teachers should ask reliable but typical students how long it has taken them to complete their homework assignment for the previous day. Sometimes the best intentioned and most sincere teachers require much more of a student's time on homework than they think they require or intend to require – a point that research supports.

For Parents

Parents, we believe, have every right to expect some general, schoolwide homework policies. This is one of the reasons we suggest that such policies be established. Likewise, we feel parents should hold teachers responsible for planning homework that is integrated with instruction, for descriptions of long-range projects, and for class-specific explanations of the nature and frequency of homework. In our view, if general expectations regarding homework are not known in advance, then parents must press for them.

Our recommendations for parents go beyond insisting on their rights to be informed. Certainly in the most school-supportive homes, time for homework is regularly set aside and only rarely violated; there is a good environment for homework, one free from distractions and with basic resources and materials at hand; and parents themselves are on hand to offer assistance, encouragement, or monitoring as needed. Teachers in specific classes could inform parents of what kinds of at-home resources would facilitate home study (for example, dictionary, atlas, newspapers, etc.). Major project due dates can be posted on the family calendar. Efforts to help students plan in advance and budget their time from week to week and evening to evening will help instill habits valuable in both school and non-school life. At the same time, parents can avoid such scenes as those we heard described when their children announce yet-to-be-started semester projects three days before the due date. Young people, we know, "forget," sometimes all too conveniently. And often, Mom and Dad are relied on to pull them through. But oh, the price that is paid in such last minute, frustrated rushes!

We think parents should monitor the amount of homework their children actually do – or are expected to do – from week to week. When it is time to complain about or to praise a teacher's homework practices, track records are more compelling than individual incidents. Principals should hear from parents when a teacher repeatedly assigns 1½ hours of homework every night. But they should also hear from parents when a science project or an art project made sense, was well planned, was enjoyed, and was rewarding for a boy or girl.

If parents, principals, and teachers work together to improve homework policies and practices, it is likely that students' performance on homework assignments will improve, as will their attitudes toward homework. In addition to the concerted efforts of parents, teachers, and principals, students also have their responsibilities in the homework enterprise.

For Students

First, notebooks in which to record homework assignments are essential, as are end-of-day checks to make sure all books and materials for a given night's homework are taken home. Students have heard most of this before – it is common sense. More controversial is our recommendation that students inform their teachers if they find homework demands excessive. Some teachers (even good teachers) lose sight of just how long some reading assignment may take or just what is involved in listing all of the government officials in a county in one evening for the next day's class. (I promised my oldest daughter that I would include this last example – DAE.)

The teacher should be the first to know – not the last – when homework becomes drudgery. Therefore, we encourage students to talk with their teachers when homework problems arise. To counteract the all too common tendency of students to label all homework as "waste of time" or "drudgery," we suggest they consider their homework assignments individually and analyze each according to its potential merits. Students (even very young students) can begin thinking about how doing this or doing that may really help them in a class, expand their experience, or establish a knowledge base to build on later. And we encourage young people to seek such purposefulness in the assignments they are given.

Finally, we would recommend to students that they should expect to have a reasonable amount of homework and should understand that not all homework will be easy. If properly approached, students should not have to question the benefits of school work done at home. But our suspicion is that since homework has been so improperly approached for so long, there will continue to be many questions and complaints from all four of the groups concerned.

Homework Do's and Don'ts

The following homework do's and don'ts provide a quick summary of the points covered in the preceding narrative. Our lists are selective but not mutually exclusive. We have tried to limit our admonitions to those few we feel would really matter if heeded.

For Principals:

1. **Do not** believe everything you hear about a teacher's homework practices.
2. **Do not** expect all teachers to be equally enthusiastic about a schoolwide homework policy.
3. **Do not** expect a schoolwide homework policy to please all parents.
4. **Do not** expect teachers with the heaviest instructional loads to assign as much homework as those with the lightest loads.
5. **Do** check out all rumors that come your way about teachers' homework practices.
6. **Do** put the teachers you least expect to be pleased by a schoolwide homework policy on the committee that formulates it.
7. **Do** involve parents in the development of schoolwide homework policies.
8. **Do** everything possible to assist teachers with managing homework paper loads, including use of school aides and parent volunteers.

For Teachers:

1. **Do not** ever give homework as punishment.
2. **Do not** make up spur-of-the-moment homework assignments.
3. **Do not** assume that because there are no questions asked about a homework assignment that students have no questions about the assignment.
4. **Do not** expect students (even your best students) always to have their homework assignments completed.
5. **Do** understand that not all types of homework assignments are equally valuable for all types of students.
6. **Do** explain the specific purpose of every homework assignment.

7. **Do** listen to what students say about their experiences in completing your homework assignments.
8. **Do** acknowledge and be thankful for efforts students make to complete their homework.

For Parents:

1. **Do** make sure your child really needs help before offering to help with homework.
2. **Do** help your child see a purpose or some value in homework assignments.
3. **Do** encourage your children to complete assignments after absences from school.
4. **Do** suggest an alternative to watching TV on nights when no homework is assigned, such as sharing a magazine article, enjoying a game together, or going to an exhibit or concert.
5. **Do not** try to help with homework if you are confused and really cannot figure out what is expected.
6. **Do not** hesitate to have your child explain legitimate reasons for nights when homework simply cannot be completed.
7. **Do not** place yourself in an adversarial role between your child and teachers over homework issues until all other alternatives are exhausted.
8. **Do not** feel your child always has to be doing "something productive." (There are few things sadder than a burned-out 14-year-old.)

For Students:

1. **Do** ask your parents for help with your homework only when you really need help.
2. **Do** ask the teacher for help before or after class if you are confused about a homework assignment.
3. **Do** explain to teachers legitimate reasons that sometimes make it impossible to complete some homework assignments.
4. **Do** make every effort to complete homework assignments when they are very important for a particular class.

5. **Do not** expect that your parents will be able to help with all your homework. (Parents forget things they have learned, and some of what is taught in school today is foreign to adults.)
6. **Do not** ask teachers to help with any homework assignment you really can complete independently.
7. **Do not** confuse *excuses* for incomplete homework assignments with legitimate *reasons*.
8. **Do not** think doing your homework "most of the time" will be satisfactory for those classes where homework counts the most. (In such classes, even a 75% completion rate may not be enough.)

Some Questions We Should Be Asking About Homework

Given the entrenched position of homework as a school tradition, it is not likely that research will markedly or quickly influence practice. Still, as analyses of effective schools continue and as we learn more about variables influencing student achievement, more attention to homework seems justified. Indeed, such attention is long overdue.

Initially, of course, we need much more and much better information on the effects of homework on student performance and achievement. Future research efforts on homework effectiveness need to be much more specific than those completed to date. For example, what types of assignments are appropriate at particular grade levels and how much is worthwhile for children at different developmental levels? What happens when homework assignments are matched with students' learning styles? What types of homework yield the greatest benefits in particular courses or types of courses?

Teachers' motives in assigning and responding to homework warrant much more research. What types of teachers assign the most homework? What kinds of assignments are particular types of teachers most likely to assign? And, as always, we need to be exploring *why*.

Given recent concern with better teacher evaluation, we should know how the amounts and types of homework teachers assign influence perceptions of their general performance. What relationships exist between homework practices and how teachers judge each other, and how they are judged by parents, administrators, and students? And how does the amount and the types of homework assigned influence public attitudes toward particular schools?

There is still much to be explored before we can speak confidently about variables that influence the completion of homework. Do these variables change from one type of homework assignment to another? Why is it that some students do homework assignments more consistently and conscientiously than others? As basic as these questions may seem, our answers to them thus far tend to be ambiguous and general.

These brief observations suggest only some of the potential research possibilities still to be explored. Such questions may lead to other questions, with the ultimate goal of research translated into better homework policies and practices.

Without such research, homework is likely to continue as it has in the past – and remain as one of the most pervasive yet relatively unexamined practices in our schools. Homework will continue, sometimes for its own sake. Assignments will be made in a hurry and completed without much purpose. And, unfortunately, whatever meaningful contributions sensible homework practices might make will be lost in the glut of uninformed, unreasonable, and even *silly* homework assignments common in almost all schools.

For all we know for sure, many teachers may be wasting a great deal of time, energy, and effort. Parents may be grumbling about too much or too little homework, when it matters much less than they have been led to believe. And children may be wasting large portions of their youth.

At the very least, when considering "homework – and why," we need to open our minds and our eyes to homework realities. Thereafter, we should be able to proceed with greater confidence in the fact that homework is justified and that it can make sense to all involved.

Bibliography

Bond, G.W., and Smith, G.J. "Homework in the Elementary School." *National Elementary Principal* 45, no. 3 (1966): 46-50.

Cartledge, C.M., and Sasser, J.E. *The Effect of Homework Assignments on the Mathematics Achievement of College Students in Freshman Algebra.* 1981. (ERIC Document Reproduction Service No. ED 206 495)

Check, J.F. "Homework: Is It Needed?" *The Clearing House* 41 (1966): 143-47.

Coulter, J.F. *Secondary School Homework.* Education Department of Western Australia Cooperative Research Study Report No. 7. Australia: Education Department of Western Australia, 1980.

Friesen, C.D. "The Results of Homework Versus No Homework Research Studies." Paper presented at the University of Iowa, 1979. (Eric Document Reproduction Service No. ED 167 508)

Harding, C. "The Relationship of Teacher Attitudes Toward Homework and the Achievement of Primary Grade Children." Doctoral dissertation, Lehigh University, 1979.

Hedges, W.D. "Guidelines for Developing a Homework Policy." *National Elementary Principal* 45, no. 2 (1964): 44-47.

Kerzic, R.L. "Value of Homework." *The Clearing House* 41 (1966): 140-42.

Knorr, C.L. "A Synthesis of Homework Research and Related Literature." Paper presented to the Lehigh Chapter of Phi Delta Kappa in Bethlehem, Pa., 1981. (Eric Document Reproduction Service No. ED 199 933)

Kohr, R.L. "The Relationship of Homework and Television Viewing to Cognitive Student Outcomes." Paper presented at the annual meeting of the National Council for Measurement in Education in San Francisco, 1979.

LaConte, R.T. *Homework as a Learning Experience: What Research Says to the Teacher.* Washington, D.C.: National Education Association, 1981. (Eric Document Reproduction Service No. ED 217 022)

Wildman, P.R. "Homework Pressures." *Peabody Journal of Education* 45 (1968): 202-204.

Bibliography

Bond, [illegible] and [illegible] "Homework [illegible] the [illegible]" [illegible] (1983): [illegible]

Coulter, [illegible] [illegible] (ERIC Document Reproduction Service No. ED 178 [illegible])

[illegible] Pruitt [illegible] (1979) [illegible]

[illegible] New York [illegible]

[illegible] Document Reproduction Service No. [illegible]

Friesen, C. D. "The Results of Homework Versus No-Homework Research Studies." [illegible] Iowa City, 1979. (ERIC Document Reproduction Service No. ED 167 508)

[illegible] "The Relationship [illegible] Homework [illegible] Achievement [illegible] (1982): [illegible]

[illegible] (1960): [illegible]

Keith, T. Z. "Time Spent on Homework [illegible]" (1982): [illegible]

Knorr, C. L. "A Synthesis of Homework Research and Related Literature." Paper presented to the [illegible] Chapter of Phi Delta Kappa, Bethlehem, [illegible] (ERIC Document Reproduction Service No. ED 199 933)

[illegible] "The Relationship of [illegible] Homework, and Television Viewing to Cognitive Student Outcomes." Paper presented at the annual meeting of the National Council for Measurement in Education, San Francisco, 1979.

LaConte, R. T. Homework as a Learning Experience: What Research Says to the Teacher. Washington, D.C.: National Education Association, 1981. (ERIC Document Reproduction Service No. ED 217 022)

Wildman, P. R. "Homework Pressures." Peabody Journal of Education 45 (1968): 202-204.